HAL•LEONARD® RECORDER SONGBOOK

Kids' Songs

ISBN 978-1-4234-9297-9

HAL•LEONARD®
CORPORATION
7777 W. BLUEMOUND RD. P.O. BOX 13819 MILWAUKEE, WI 53213

Visit Hal Leonard Online at
www.halleonard.com

THE ADDAMS FAMILY THEME

Theme from the TV Show and Movie

RECORDER

Music and Lyrics by
VIC MIZZY

ALLEY CAT SONG

RECORDER

Words by JACK HARLEN
Music by FRANK BJORN

THE CANDY MAN

from WILLY WONKA AND THE CHOCOLATE FACTORY

RECORDER

Words and Music by LESLIE BRICUSSE
and ANTHONY NEWLEY

EVERYTHING IS BEAUTIFUL

RECORDER

Words and Music by
RAY STEVENS

THE HOKEY POKEY

RECORDER

Words and Music by CHARLES P. MACAK,
TAFFT BAKER and LARRY LaPRISE

I WHISTLE A HAPPY TUNE

from THE KING AND I

RECORDER

Lyrics by OSCAR HAMMERSTEIN II
Music by RICHARD RODGERS

PETER COTTONTAIL

RECORDER

Words and Music by STEVE NELSON
and JACK ROLLINS

PUFF THE MAGIC DRAGON

RECORDER

Words and Music by LENNY LIPTON
and PETER YARROW

Moderately

SESAME STREET THEME

RECORDER

Words by BRUCE HART,
JON STONE and JOE RAPOSO
Music by JOE RAPOSO

SING

from SESAME STREET

RECORDER

Words and Music by
JOE RAPOSO

TAKE ME OUT TO THE BALL GAME

from TAKE ME OUT TO THE BALL GAME

RECORDER

Words by JACK NORWORTH
Music by ALBERT VON TILZER

THIS LAND IS YOUR LAND

Words and Music by
WOODY GUTHRIE

RECORDER

WON'T YOU BE MY NEIGHBOR?

(It's a Beautiful Day in the Neighborhood)

from MISTER ROGERS' NEIGHBORHOOD

Words and Music by
FRED ROGERS

RECORDER